I0616137

The STRAIT WAY *to* HEAVEN

The STRAIT
WAY *to*
HEAVEN

Twenty Precious Directions for Your Souls

WILLIAM DYER
Revised & Updated by Ron Metheny

We enjoy hearing from our readers. Please contact us at www.anekopress.com/questions-comments with any questions, comments, or suggestions.

Cover Designer: J. Lewis

Editor: Ron Metheny, R. Clark

Aneko Press

www.anekopress.com

Aneko Press, Life Sentence Publishing, and our logos are trademarks of

Life Sentence Publishing, Inc.
203 E. Birch Street
P.O. Box 652
Abbotsford, WI 54405

RELIGION / Christian Living / Spiritual Growth

Paperback ISBN: 979-8-88936-485-6

eBook ISBN: 979-8-88936-486-3

10   9   8   7   6   5   4   3   2   1

Available where books are sold

Contents

Principles of the Revised Text

1. The basis of this revision is the definitive text of *The Strait Way to Heaven* as written and published by William Dyer in the late seventeenth century (exact date unknown).

2. Of foremost consideration has been a style of simple conversational (modern-American) English that maintains faithfulness to the design, meaning, doctrine, and purpose of the Puritan preacher William Dyer who lived, preached, and wrote in England during the time of the English Civil Wars (1642–1651), Cromwell's Protectorate (1649–1659), and the restoration of the monarchy under King Charles II (reign 1660–1685).

3. The majority of linguistic archaisms have been modified to produce a more contemporary style of expression, while other select antiquated modes of vocabulary, sentence structure, punctuation, etc. have

been retained, since these have gained a particularly timeless quality and quaintness about them that are seemingly intrinsic to *The Strait Way to Heaven.*

4. The English Standard Version is the preferred Scripture translation used in this revision, although, where deemed necessary for contextual reasons, the King James Version or the Christian Standard Bible has also been used.

5. Supplemental Scripture passages (originally quoted in full by the author) at the start of select chapters have been condensed to Scripture references in footnotes, as a courtesy to today's readers.

6. A previously published compilation of sayings of William Dyer has also been revised or updated into modern English and included as an APPENDIX to this edition.

7. Finally, in regard to these principles of the updated edition's revised text (as listed above), this editor welcomes suggestions and constructive criticism.

—Ron Metheny

Biographical Introduction

William Dyer (1632–1696)

William Dyer was born in England in 1632. During his early ministry (circa 1650s), he was a pastor with the Church of England at Chesham and then Cholesbury in Buckinghamshire. Despite having received these overtly Anglican appointments, young Dyer had apparently taken up the nonconformist (Calvinistic) mantle at the start of his gospel ministry. He and many other such nonconforming pastors were widely regarded as Puritans because of their desire to purify and reform the state church.

However, in 1662, thousands of these Puritan pastors were expelled from their pulpits in the Great Ejection – which followed the Act of Uniformity of 1662, passed by Parliament during the reign of King Charles II (1630–1685; reign 1660–1685) – because of a lack of compliance to the new policies of the established church. William Dyer lost his parish employment at this time and turned to liturgical writing instead of preaching.

In the year following the Great Ejection, Dyer wrote two of his most enduring books, *A Cabinet of Jewels, Or, A Glimpse of Sion's Glory* (1663), and *Christ's Famous Titles* (1663). Within the next two decades, many others of his written works were published in England, including among them *The Strait Way to Heaven: Twenty Precious Directions for Your Souls* (circa 1670s or 1680s; precise date unknown).

In Dyer's later life he reportedly worked alongside the Quakers and embraced some of their beliefs – in particular, their zeal for Christ and passion for souls. He died in 1696 at the age of sixty-four, and was buried in a Quaker cemetery in Southwark, England.

Though today few personal details concerning William Dyer's life and ministry exist, from his still extant writings he is clearly seen to have been a person of great piety and character, earnest to win unsaved people to the Lord, and eager to build up Christians in the love and confidence of Christ. Below is just one of many such examples:

> *"Holiness is the only way to happiness. We must not dress ourselves for the heavenly world by the mirror of this vile world."*[1]

—Ron Metheny
January 3, 2025

---

1 See chapter 15, page 29.

Chapter 1

Loathe Sin and Leave Sin

Whoever conceals his transgressions will not prosper, but he who confesses and forsakes them will obtain mercy. (Proverbs 28:13)

Before there can be a falling *off* from our sins, there must first be a falling *out* with our sins. There must be a loathing of sin in our devotions. Oh, is it not a thousand times better to part with sin – though ever so sweet – than to part with God, and Christ, and heaven? You must part with one of them! One sin will damn a soul that is *out* of Christ, but no sin can damn a soul that is *in* Christ. Sin is the evil of evils! Sin is worse than the devil, since it was sin that made the devil to be a devil.

Oh! The love of sin, and the lack of grace will ruin and destroy our souls forever. It is better not to be, than to be an unrepentant sinner! Oh, therefore kill sin so that sin does not kill you. Mourn for sin, and flee from sin. Do not commit new sins, but repent of old sins. *Then you will remember your evil ways, and your deeds that were not good, and you will loathe yourselves for your iniquities and your abominations* (Ezekiel 36:31).

Oh, poor soul, have you not served the flesh and the devil long enough? Yes! Have you not had enough of sin? Is sin so good to you, or is it so beneficial for you? Oh, what type of place will you soon be in – one of joy or torment? Oh, what sights will you soon see – in heaven or hell? Oh, what thoughts will soon fill your hearts – with unspeakable delight or horror? In what work will you be employed – to praise the Lord with Christians and angels, or to cry out in unquenchable fire with demons?

Oh, therefore die unto sin, confess it, mourn over it, and be ashamed of it; hate and loathe it, and flee from it just as you would from a venomous snake; and though your sins are more than you can count, yet they are not more than God can pardon. *If we confess our sins, he is faithful and just to forgive us our sins and to cleanse us from all unrighteousness* (1 John 1:9).

Chapter 2

Put Off the Old Self, and Put On the New Self

Do not lie to one another, seeing that you have put off the old self with its practices and have put on the new self, which is being renewed in knowledge after the image of its creator (Colossians 3:9-10).[2]

The *new self* is not what he was before; he has new understanding, a new will, new desires, new love, new entertainments, new thoughts, new words, new company, and a new life.

Oh, dear friends, be new creatures so that you may be glorious creatures. We can call nothing *ours* in heaven until Christ is *ours*. Without regeneration, there is no salvation. *"Truly, I say to you, unless you turn and*

---

2   See also 2 Corinthians 5:17; Galatians 6:15; Ephesians 4:24; and 1 Peter 2:2.

become like children, you will never enter the kingdom of heaven" (Matthew 18:3). *"Truly, truly, I say to you, unless one is born again he cannot see the kingdom of God"* (John 3:3). You have heard a lot of God, Christ, and heaven with your ears, but this will not bring you to heaven unless you have a lot of God, Christ, and heaven in your hearts!

You must be able to say, "I was once a slave of Satan, but now I am a son of God! I was once dead, but now I am alive! I was once darkness, but now I am light in the Lord! I was once a child of wrath, an heir of hell, but now I am an heir of heaven! I was once under the spirit of bondage, but now I am under the spirit of adoption." A true believer lives:

- *in* the Lord (see 1 Thessalonians 1:1),

- *by* the Lord (see Romans 1:17 and Luke 20:8),

- *on* the Lord (see John 6:57),

- *to* the Lord (see Romans 14:8), and

- *with* the Lord (see 2 Corinthians 13:4).

Chapter 3

Make Your Peace with the Prince of Peace

*For to us a child is born, to us a son is given;
and the government shall be upon his shoulder, and his name shall be called Wonderful
Counselor, Mighty God, Everlasting Father,
Prince of Peace.* (Isaiah 9:6)

*O*h, *do not lift your hands against God's Son; but
kiss the Son, lest he be angry, and you perish in
the way, for his wrath is quickly kindled. Blessed are all
who take refuge in him* (Psalm 2:12). Let:

- His will be your rule,

- His Spirit be your guide,

- His precepts be your practices,

- His decrees be your delights, and

- His chosen ones be your best companions.

Submit to His gospel and government. Oh, everyone, make your peace with God! There is a fourfold peace:

1. First, there is an external peace, that is, peace with humankind.

2. Secondly, there is a supernal peace, that is, peace with God.

3. Thirdly, there is an internal peace, that is, peace with your conscience.

4. Fourthly, there is an eternal peace, and that is, peace in heaven.

Mark the blameless and behold the upright, for there is a future for the man of peace (Psalm 37:37). If you have peace with God, then the world and the devil cannot hurt you. Believers have God for their guide and gain. He who messes with the saints of God assaults God Himself. *He who touches you touches the apple of his eye* (Zechariah 2:8). He who lifts up his hand against them, lifts up his hand against God. Though they have many enemies, yet they have one Friend who has more strength than all their enemies.

A ragged Christian is dearer to God than a glittering emperor who lacks grace. Oh, make your peace with the Prince of Peace, so that in this life you will have the assurance of eternal life, and in the next life eternal death will not be your inheritance.

Chapter 4

Make Holiness Your Main Business, and Not a Side Business

Therefore, brothers, be all the more diligent to confirm your calling and election, for if you practice these qualities you will never fall (2 Peter 1:10).[3]

O h, why is so much attention paid to the glory of this poor world? Is it not because so little attention is given to the glory of heaven? Oh, what is an earthly kingdom in comparison with the heavenly kingdom? The angels themselves, even though they are glorious spirits, yet they are ministering spirits.

Is it not true that most people of the world make light of God, and of Christ, and of the Holy Spirit, and of heaven, and of their precious souls?

"The kingdom of heaven may be compared to a

3   See also Matthew 6:33 and Philippians 2:12.

king who gave a wedding feast for his son, and sent his servants to call those who were invited to the wedding feast, but they would not come. Again he sent other servants, saying, 'Tell those who are invited, "See, I have prepared my dinner, my oxen and my fat calves have been slaughtered, and everything is ready. Come to the wedding feast."' But they paid no attention and went off, one to his farm, another to his business, while the rest seized his servants, treated them shamefully, and killed them." (Matthew 22:2-6).

Miserable worldlings make religion a side business; they will hear, read, and pray when they have nothing else to do. Oh, if only such people knew what everlasting glory and everlasting torments are! Would they then do just as they do now? Oh, that they only knew the worth of their souls, and their need for a Savior; the shortness of their time, and the greatness of their work! Would they then neglect God and their own souls like they do?

Oh, friends, let me ask you to whom I write to make holiness your main business. Make hearing, reading, praying, believing, and doing your main business. *"Do not work for the food that perishes, but for the food that endures to eternal life, which the Son of Man will give to you. For on him God the Father has set his seal"* (John 6:27).

Chapter 5

Do Nothing in This World Except That Which You Can Answer for in the Eternal World

For we must all appear before the judgment seat of Christ, so that each one may receive what is due for what he has done in the body, whether good or evil (2 Corinthians 5:10).[4]

O h! For the Lord's sake, my dear brothers, let nothing be done by you in this world except that which can be answered for in the eternal world! Many people do in this world that which they cannot answer for in the eternal world. At this moment, they despise God, blaspheme God, rebel against God, break faith with God, and persecute the beloved people of God. Instead of protecting Christians, they imprison them. They are more about crushing them than comforting

---

4   See also Ecclesiastes 12:14; Acts 17:31; and Romans 2:16.

them. Instead of visiting them, they vilify them. And instead of being affectionate towards them, they afflict them. They eat them up as they eat bread (cf. Psalm 14:4), and will not allow them to worship the true God, in spirit and in truth. Instead, they despise, mock, persecute, banish, and kill them (cf. Hebrews 11). They:

- *threaten* them (Acts 4:29),

- *accuse* them (Acts 24:5),

- *slander* them (Matthew 5:11),

- *curse* them (Matthew 5:44 AKJV),

- *beat* them (Acts 5:40),

- *imprison* them (Acts 4:3),

- *rob* them (Hebrews 10:34), and

- *murder* them (Romans 8:36).

Poor innocent Christians suffer all of this – swearing, cursing, robbing, blasphemy, gluttony, drunkenness, fornication, and every form of debauchery; yes, murder itself walks unpunished in the streets. And only he who departs from evil is prey. It is no wonder, then, that these ungodly ones will one day hide themselves in dens and holes, and *[call] to the mountains and rocks, "Fall on us and hide us from the face of him who is seated on the throne, and from the wrath of the Lamb"* (Revelation 6:15-16). Oh, what persecutors will do *when the Lord Jesus is revealed from heaven with his mighty angels in flaming fire, inflicting vengeance on those who do not know God and on those who do not obey the gospel of our Lord Jesus. They will suffer the punishment of eternal destruction, away from the presence of the Lord and from the glory of his might* (2 Thessalonians 1:7-9). Will they not be awestruck and speechless – not a single word to say for themselves, just like that man who did not have a wedding garment on (cf. Matthew 22:12)?

But oh, beloved, let that *grace of God [that] has appeared, bringing salvation for all people, [train] us to renounce ungodliness and worldly passions, and to live self-controlled, upright, and godly lives in the present age* (Titus 2:11-12), following the Lamb, resisting Satan, abstaining from sin, and separating ourselves from the world.

Chapter 6

The Word of God Is the Christian's Rule, and the Spirit of God Is the Christian's Guide

To the teaching and to the testimony! If they will not speak according to this word, it is because they have no dawn (Isaiah 8:20).[5]

Most people walk by false rules:

1. Some walk by popular opinion.

2. Some walk by worldly customs.

3. Some walk by fate.

4. Some walk by conscience.

5. Some walk by their own logic.

6. Some walk by other people's examples.

7. Some walk by their own lusts.

But oh, my dear friends, let me ask you to walk by none

---

5   See also John 16:13; 2 Timothy 3:16; and 2 Peter 2:19.

of these false rules. Instead, keep close to the Word and Spirit of God.

Scripture is a rule outside of us, to show us where we must go; the Spirit is a guide inside of us, to enable us to walk according to the direction of that Word. The Word of God is a compass, by which we must direct our journey; the Spirit is the great captain, who steers us on this journey. We have no eyes to see the Word until the Spirit enlightens them. We have no ears to hear the Word until the Spirit opens them. We have no hearts to obey the Word until the Spirit presses down and prepares them.

By the Word of God, we know the mind of the Spirit of God. And by the effectiveness of the Spirit, we feel the power of the Word. The Word of God shows us the way, and the Spirit of God leads us in the way that the Word points out. The Spirit of God is able to expound the Word of God and make it easy for us to understand. The Holy Spirit is the Christian's interpreter; He gives Scripture, and He alone can reveal unto us the sense and meaning of Scripture.

The Word is God's counsel that reveals the path in which we are to walk; the Spirit is God's Counselor who teaches us how to walk in that path. The Word is a mirror that shows us our duty. If God had not put His Spirit into our hearts, as well as His Word into our heads, we never would have arrived at the safe harbor of peace.

Scripture reveals the precise heart of God. As it was, in Holy Scripture, God Almighty has manifested Himself; He has unveiled all His counsel to human beings, as far as is necessary to be known, for their direction and guidance to everlasting life.

Chapter 7

Be Faithful and Fruitful

Therefore, my beloved brothers, be steadfast, immovable, always abounding in the work of the Lord, knowing that in the Lord your labor is not in vain. (1 Corinthians 15:58)

"*E*very tree that does not bear good fruit is cut down and thrown into the fire*"* (Matthew 7:19). Christians must be fruitful, and not lazy. Make sure that you bear good fruit – and a lot of it. But what is *good fruit*?

First, it is *sincerity,* which is not a specific virtue, but is the mind of all virtues. *Behold, you delight in truth in the inward being* (Psalm 51:6).

Secondly, it is *humility,* which is the virtue most successful with God in obtaining all other virtues. *"Take my yoke upon you and learn from me, because*

I am lowly and humble in heart, and you will find rest for your souls" (Matthew 11:29 CSB).

Thirdly, it is *prudence.* The patient Christian is best at waiting, but the prudent Christian is best at working. *"Be wise as serpents and innocent as doves"* (Matthew 10:16). We must have innocence with our wisdom, or else our wisdom is just wiliness. And we must have wisdom with our innocence, or else our innocence is just weakness. We must have the purity of doves, so that we will not harm others, and we must have the prudence of serpents, so that others will not abuse and take advantage of us. Not to wrong the truth by silence – here is the innocence of doves; not to betray ourselves by rashness – here is the wisdom of serpents.

Fourthly, it is *patience. Here is a call for the endurance of the saints, those who keep the commandments of God and their faith in Jesus* (Revelation 14:12). The way to bring the world under our control is to be patient under its frowns. Be faithful in your promises and in your purposes. Be faithful to the ways of God and His gospel cause. Oh, do not start with the Lamb, and end with the beast, but *"be faithful unto death, and I will give you the crown of life"* (Revelation 2:10). Have your lamps lit, and your consciences awakened; be dressed for action – in clean apparel, and with your spiritual armor constantly on!

Lastly, it is *self-denial. "If anyone would come after me, let him deny himself and take up his cross and follow me"* (Matthew 16:24).

Chapter 8

Beware of Believing the World's Report concerning God's People

When Ahab saw Elijah, Ahab said to him, "Is it you, you troubler of Israel?" (1 Kings 18:17)

Those who have a good conscience do not always have a good reputation. The people of God in this life are called by the wicked *troublemakers, rebels, anarchists,* and what not. This is an old tactic of that old Serpent – to impute the troubles of the nation upon God's Elijahs.

Jeremiah was deemed worthy of death for speaking against Judah's sins and wickedness, and for denouncing God's judgments against them. *And when Jeremiah had finished speaking all that the LORD had commanded him to speak to all the people, then the priests and the prophets and all the people laid hold of him, saying, "You shall die!"* (Jeremiah 26:8).

Also in Jeremiah 38:4 it says, *Then the officials said to the king, "Let this man be put to death, for he is weakening the hands of the soldiers who are left in this city, and the hands of all the people, by speaking such words to them. For this man is not seeking the welfare of this people, but their harm."*

Also with Amos – for speaking against the abominations of the king's court, Amos is charged with treason against the king's character. *Then Amaziah the priest of Bethel sent to Jeroboam king of Israel, saying, "Amos has conspired against you in the midst of the house of Israel. The land is not able to bear all his words." And Amaziah said to Amos, "O seer, go, flee away to the land of Judah, and eat bread there, and prophesy there"* (Amos 7:10, 12).

Also Paul and Silas were accused by both the envious Jews and the lewd plebeians of turning the world upside down, and breaking the decrees of Caesar, for preaching up the kingly power of Jesus Christ. Indeed, Christ Himself was accused of the same. Take note of what the Jews said about Him: *And they began to accuse him, saying, "We found this man misleading our nation and forbidding us to give tribute to Caesar, and saying that he himself is Christ, a king"* (Luke 23:2). And for this the servants of God in every era have been accused and persecuted, killed and stoned (cf. Matthew 23:37). Now, if the Lord and Master was called an enemy of

Caesar, no wonder those of His own household are called the same. Our integrity will not protect us from infamy! The best among all Christians have had black marks in the world's history. It is customary for those who live in treason and rebellion against the King of heaven to slander His servants with treason and rebellion against the kings of earth.

But, my dear brothers, be aware of this: Just as the deaths of Christians are precious in the Lord's sight, so are their reputations (cf. Psalm 116:15). The world will invent a hundred lies against God's people. *"Others [will] revile you and persecute you and utter all kinds of evil against you falsely on my account"* (Matthew 5:11; see also 1 Peter 4:14). Wicked people hate those most whom God loves most! But God will wipe away the blemishes from His people; He will cause their innocence and righteousness to shine like the noonday sun, and their reputations will be forever remembered. Yes, on that great day, God will clear their innocence before humanity, angels, and all the world.

Chapter 9

Stay In with God When People Fall Out with You

But for me it is good to be near God; I have made the Lord God my refuge, that I may tell of all Your works (Psalm 73:28).[6]

This is a great comfort to God's people – though they are like lilies among thorns, and like sheep among wolves, they have a God to go to! *Come, my people, enter your chambers, and shut your doors behind you; hide yourselves for a little while until the fury has passed by* (Isaiah 26:20).

Let the world frown, and friends forsake you; God can sweeten all your enjoyments. Stay within God's way, and you will be sure of God's protection; keep God's precepts, and God will keep you. Do what God commands and avoid what God forbids, and you will

6   See also Psalm 91:10-11; Proverbs 18:10; Habakkuk 3:18; and James 4:8.

have no need to fear what humankind can do to you. If you want God to take care of you, you must cast your care upon Him; wait on Him, walk with Him, obey His precepts, and believe His promises.

Oh, beloved, let wicked people fall out with us, hate us, and slander us as much as they will; they cannot hurt us if we stay in with God. Therefore, my beloved, above all else, fellowship with God, and *stay* in fellowship with Him. All Christians will enjoy heaven when they leave earth; some Christians enjoy heaven while they are on earth. Fellowship with God will provide you with two heavens: a heaven on earth, and a heaven after death! He enjoys nothing who does not enjoy fellowship with God.

Chapter 10

Live Above the Love of Life
and the Fear of Death

*"For whoever would save his life will lose it,
but whoever loses his life for my sake will
find it* (Matthew 16:25).[7]

W hoever loves Christ more than his life will be
sure to save and keep both. Whoever goes out
of God's way to avoid dangers will certainly encounter
danger.

My dear friends, let us live *above* sufferings and
fears – even though we cannot live *without* sufferings.
*"In the world you will have tribulation. But take heart; I
have overcome the world"* (John 16:33). Whoever loves
Christ above life will let *life* go rather than *Christ.*

My beloved, consider Christ and the *cloud of wit-
nesses* (Hebrews 12:1) and martyrs who have gone before

---

7   See also Luke 14:26 and 1 Corinthians 6:19-20.

us, and passed over through all these floods, and safely arrived to shore; who are now in heaven with God and Christ, where *there is fullness of joy* and *pleasures forevermore* (Psalm 16:11). Oh, the joy that they enjoy! Oh, the rivers of consolation that flow from God! *"They are before the throne of God, and serve him day and night in his temple; and he who sits on the throne will shelter them with his presence. They shall hunger no more, neither thirst anymore; the sun shall not strike them, nor any scorching heat. For the Lamb in the midst of the throne will be their shepherd, and he will guide them to springs of living water, and God will wipe away every tear from their eyes"* (Revelation 7:15-17).

Who are these who will have all this honor, glory, joy, and blessedness in heaven? For this, see Revelation 7:14. *"These are the ones coming out of the great tribulation. They have washed their robes and made them white in the blood of the Lamb."* The sweetness of the crown that believers will receive will make amends for the bitterness of the cross that they have carried.

Chapter 11

Desire Better Hearts More
Than Better Times

O Jerusalem, wash your heart from evil, that
you may be saved. How long shall your wicked
thoughts lodge within you? (Jeremiah 4:14).[8]

O h, beloved, instead of reforming ourselves, we
are complaining about wicked people! We complain about their wickedness more than our apostasy!
We complain about their offenses against us more than
our offenses against God. For a long time we have been
sinning, and for a long time we need to be repenting.
But the times would not have been so bad if we had
not been so bad; the times would soon be better if we
were only better.

Unfortunately, beloved, we have committed those
sins that unrighteous people could not commit! We

---

8   See also Jeremiah 17:9 and Matthew 15:19.

have sinned against the brightest light and dearest love! The better God has been to us, the worse we have been to Him! He has loaded us with His mercies, and we have wearied Him with our sins. Oh, let us blame ourselves more, and the times less. Let us turn unto the Lord so that He may turn unto us in love and mercy. Let our hearts go out to Him so that His heart may come unto us.

Oh, beg and plead for better hearts, so that you may serve God better! Beg for broken hearts and for sincere hearts, since it is the heart that God looks at and calls for. *My son, give me your heart* (Proverbs 23:26). Our hearts are always out of tune to serve God, but never out of tune to serve sin, since if we had ever so good times, and not good hearts, it would hurt us rather than bless us.

Chapter 12

Grow Downward in Humility and Inward in Sincerity

*"Whoever exalts himself will be humbled,
and whoever humbles himself will be exalted*
(Matthew 23:12).[9]

Be low in your own eyes, and keep a low self-esteem; despise pride, and flee from it; be inwardly sincere, as well as outwardly humble; do not look heavenward by your profession, and hellward by your conversation. Whoever lives in sin is dead in sin (cf. Ephesians 2:1). *Grace be with all them that love our Lord Jesus Christ in sincerity* (Ephesians 6:24 AKJV). Let your hearts be upright with God, and walk as those who have God as their inheritance, knowing there are many eyes on you: the eye of God, the eye of Christ, the eye of angels, the eye of Christians, the eye of the world, and the devil's

---

9   See also Ephesians 3:8; Colossians 3:12; and 1 Peter 5:5-6.

eye also! Therefore, walk wisely and sincerely; be like the king's daughter, *all glorious within* – though within is not all her glory, for her robes are *interwoven with gold* (Psalm 45:13).

Do you think you are good just because others think so? Unfortunately, the best people's confidence in us is poor evidence of heaven. Instead, the best testimony is that which is within us and above us. Therefore, see that you grow in grace, and delight in holiness, bear a lot of fruit, and live quietly before the living God. Beware of hypocrisy; make it your daily business to walk with God; practice humility a lot, for humility will truly enhance your profession. Do not put in a few good words for religion when the substance is neglected, but live as you would die; live today as if you were to die tomorrow.

Chapter 13

Do Good to Those Who Are Good

Do not neglect to do good and to share what you have, for such sacrifices are pleasing to God (Hebrews 13:16).[10]

There are many people who have a whole lot of this world's wealth, riches, and goods in their hands and in their houses, but have no grace in their hearts. And therefore, they do no good with the goods of this world. They live so unfaithfully that their lives are barely worth a prayer, and their deaths barely worth a tear. People may as well go to hell for not doing good as for doing evil. Whoever bears no good fruit is just as much fuel for hell as the one who bears bad fruit.

You may not be outwardly bad, and yet are not inwardly good. You may be as far from grace as from vice. The rich glutton was in hell's torments, not for

---

10   See also Micah 6:8; 1 Timothy 6:18; Hebrews 13:3; and James 1:27.

persecuting Lazarus, but for not relieving Lazarus (cf. Luke 16:25). *"For I was hungry and you gave me no food, I was thirsty and you gave me no drink"* (Matthew 25:42).

"Curse Meroz, says the angel of the Lord, curse its inhabitants thoroughly, because they did not come to the help of the Lord, to the help of the Lord against the mighty" (Judges 5:23). It is one of the greatest mercies in the world for God to give a person a heart to do good with the good that He has given him.

Oh, beloved, always be doing good and hating evil. Do not look only where you may *get* good for yourself, but also where you may *do* good to others. Work to be helpful to the souls of others, and supply the needs of others.

Chapter 14

Choose Suffering over Sinning

By faith Moses, when he was grown up, refused to be called the son of Pharaoh's daughter, choosing rather to be mistreated with the people of God than to enjoy the fleeting pleasures of sin (Hebrews 11:24-25).[11]

O h, beloved, there is more evil in the slightest sin against Christ than in the greatest suffering for Christ! *For this light momentary affliction is preparing for us an eternal weight of glory beyond all comparison* (2 Corinthians 4:17).

1. Our sufferings for Christ are rather light.

2. Our sufferings for Christ are short – just for a moment.

3. Christ stands by us in our sufferings.

---

11   See also Daniel 3:16-18; 6:10; Hebrews 10:34; and 11:35-37.

4. Our sufferings are ordered by the Father.

5. Our sufferings will not hurt our souls.

6. God gives us the best of comforts in the worst of times.

7. We have the most consolation from God when we have the most tribulation from people.

Just as our sufferings abound, our consolations also abound. When the burden is heaviest on the back, then the peace of conscience is sweetest and greatest within. Therefore, my dear brothers, keep yourselves out of the filthy puddle of this world, and from the evil of this world; and if you must sin or suffer, choose suffering over sinning.

Chapter 15

Do Not Think the Worse of Godliness Because It Is Frowned Upon, Nor the Better of Ungodliness Because It Is Smiled Upon

For while bodily training is of some value, godliness is of value in every way, as it holds promise for the present life and also for the life to come (1 Timothy 4:8).[12]

Oh, friends, do not think the worse of holiness because wicked people and demons criticize it, mock it, and persecute it; nor the better of wickedness because wicked people love it, follow it, and say, *"It is vain to serve God. What is the profit of our keeping his charge or of walking as in mourning before the LORD of hosts?"* (Malachi 3:14). But the time is coming when ungodly people will give all they have for that holiness

12   See also Romans 6:23; Philippians 3:8; and Ephesians 5:11.

they now despise. But they will be just as far from obtaining it as they are now from desiring it.

Therefore, let us love *the holiness without which no one will see the Lord* (Hebrews 12:14) and hate wickedness. Holiness is the only way to happiness. We must not dress ourselves for the heavenly world by the mirror of this vile world.

"You shall not fall in with the many to do evil" (Exodus 23:2). *For many, of whom I have often told you and now tell you even with tears, walk as enemies of the cross of Christ. Their end is destruction, their god is their belly, and they glory in their shame, with minds set on earthly things* (Philippians 3:18-19). The children of God must be harmless in their doings, and blameless in their goings.

Chapter 16

Cherish the Word of God Because of Its Value, So That You May Never Come to Cherish The Word of God Because of Its Lack!

How sweet are your words to my taste, sweeter than honey to my mouth! (Psalm 119:103).[13]

Oh, let us with Job value the Word of God more than our necessary food (see Job 23:12), and with David more than our gold and silver (see Psalm 119:72, 127)! The Christian's delight in God's Word exceeds all of his creature delights. Wicked people can delight in the creatures of God, but not in the Word of God. They can delight in the gifts of God, but not in the God of gifts. Oh, let us love the Word, let us cherish the Word! It is the sun of the spiritual world, just as the sun is the light of the natural world. Without the

---

13   See also Psalm 119:97; Colossians 3:16; and 1 Peter 2:2.

sun, the world is complete chaos and a dungeon full of darkness! Likewise, the Word of God is the light of the spiritual world, without which a person is in eternal night.

Take away Scripture, and there will be no explicit rule to direct people as to what must be done, or what must be believed. In Scripture, here all false ways are exposed, here all sins are forbidden, here all holiness is commanded. In Scripture, here you may see every action and motion of our lives as a step to life, or a step to death; as a step towards heaven, or a step towards hell. The Word is the savor of life unto life, unto those who believe. Oh, therefore, cherish and obey the Word!

1. It is a simple word.

2. It is a true word.

3. It is a sure word.

4. It is a powerful word.

Oh, beloved, let us read the Word and abide in the Word. *"If you abide in my word, you are truly my disciples"* (John 8:31).

Chapter 17

Beware of the Prostitute of Babylon's Golden Cup and Sweet Wine!

*The woman was arrayed in purple and scar-
let, and adorned with gold and jewels and
pearls, holding in her hand a golden cup full
of abominations and the impurities of her
sexual immorality* (Revelation 17:4).[14]

L et me ask you to beware of this and avoid this! Be
like the virgin spouse of Christ who follows Him
wherever He goes.

My dear friends, beware of and avoid four things:

First, false *teachers.*

The devil has his ministers, just like Christ. *"Beware
of false prophets, who come to you in sheep's clothing but
inwardly are ravenous wolves"* (Matthew 7:15).

---

14   See also Revelation 12:15.

Yes, they are ferocious wolves, and they can never have enough! They are false shepherds who look only after their own gain. *The dogs have a mighty appetite; they never have enough. But they are shepherds who have no understanding; they have all turned to their own way, each to his own gain, one and all* (Isaiah 56:11).

Oh! False teachers do not feed the flock, but fleece it! They do not convert, but pervert! They do not purify, but poison! They do not edify for salvation, but destroy for damnation! Instead of curing souls, they kill them!

So long as they pilfer the people's money, they do not care, though the devil has their souls. They are neither rightly called, nor rightly qualified, nor rightly ordained. *"This evil people, who refuse to hear my words, who stubbornly follow their own heart and have gone after other gods to serve them and worship them, shall be like this loincloth, which is good for nothing"* (Jeremiah 13:10). They are dogs and wolves joining together to massacre the flock of Christ. Oh! Therefore, stay away from Babylon's merchants who make merchandise of people's souls (cf. Revelation 18:10-13). Oh, the sins of teachers are the teachers of sins!

Secondly, beware of false *doctrine.*

But false prophets also arose among the people, just as there will be false teachers among you, who will secretly bring in destructive heresies, even denying the

Master who bought them, bringing upon themselves swift destruction. And many will follow their sensuality, and because of them the way of truth will be blasphemed (2 Peter 2:1-2). *Do not be led away by diverse and strange teachings* (Hebrews 13:9).

My brothers, I also exhort you in the Lord that you do not carnally comply with, nor superstitiously conform to, people's inventions. *For freedom Christ has set us free; stand firm therefore, and do not submit again to a yoke of slavery* (Galatians 5:1).

Thirdly, beware of false *worship*.

> *"If anyone worships the beast and its image and receives a mark on his forehead or on his hand, he also will drink the wine of God's wrath, poured full strength into the cup of his anger, and he will be tormented with fire and sulfur in the presence of the holy angels and in the presence of the Lamb."*
> (Revelation 14:9-10)

> *"You worship what you do not know; we worship what we know, for salvation is from the Jews. But the hour is coming, and is now here, when the true worshipers will worship the Father in spirit and truth, for the Father*

is seeking such people to worship him. God is spirit, and those who worship him must worship in spirit and truth." (John 4:22-24)

As there are some in the world who worship a false god, there are also others who worship the true God with false worship. Those who worship the beast worship the devil. Oh! Do not mess around with false worship, with vain worship, or with superstitious worship. Worship God as He teaches us to worship Him. Our work is to depend on Christ's work; our outward working is to depend on God's inward workings.

Fourthly, beware of false *opinions.*

Let your hearts be upright, your judgments be sound, and your lives be holy. Love the truth, obey the truth, and hold fast the truth.

Now, beloved, let me exhort you for God's sake, for Christ's sake, and for your soul's sake, to stay away from false teachers, from false doctrine, from false worship, and from false opinions. If you will be tasting and sipping from Babylon's golden cup, you must resolve to receive Babylon's plagues!

Chapter 18

Be One with Everyone Who
Is One with Christ

*[Be] eager to maintain the unity of the Spirit
in the bond of peace* (Ephesians 4:3).[15]

O h, consider what a dishonor it is to the gospel
that those who profess themselves to be children
of the same God, members of the same Christ, temples
of the same Spirit, and heirs of the same glory should be
fighting with one another! It is strange and unnatural
that those who are Christians in profession should be
demons in practice towards one another – that God's
diamonds should cut one another. For wolves to devour
the lambs is no wonder, but for lambs to devour one
another is astonishing and monstrous!

Oh! Many professors, instead of loving one another,
hate one another. Oh, how unlike are we to that of

---

15   See also 1 John 4:20 and 5:1.

God whom we profess to be our God. He is full of love, full of goodness, and full of mercy and patience. Oh, but Christians cannot bear and forbear with one another. Oh! Do not wicked people warm themselves by the sparks of our divisions, and say, "It is just how we would have it!"

Oh, beloved, has God not made His wrath to smoke against us for the disputes and resentments[16] that have been among us? Oh, that you would lay this to heart, and throw away discord, division, and discontent, and labor for a oneness in love and affection with everyone who is one with Christ. Oh, labor for a healing spirit.

You cannot love God if you do not love God's people. *If anyone says, "I love God," and hates his brother, he is a liar* (1 John 4:20). *Let brotherly love continue* (Hebrews 13:1). Christ's doves flock together (cf. Malachi 3:16). There are many who cannot love a person unless he is of their opinions. They cannot love a member of their church, though he is a member of Christ. Every person has a good opinion about his own opinion! But regrettably, beloved, it is not this opinion, nor that opinion, nor this way, nor that way, that will bring a person to heaven without faith in Christ; and whoever has faith in Christ has a right to all the

---

16   *Heart-burnings,* in Dyer's original text, which denoted not a medical condition as might be the suggested meaning of the term today, but a spiritual condition – that is, denoting intense *jealousy* or *resentment.*

ordinances of Christ, the promises of Christ, and the privileges of Christ.

Therefore, let me exhort you to love every godly person regardless of his minor differences from you. *Now the full number of those who believed were of one heart and soul* (Acts 4:32).

Chapter 19

Love Christ with a Love Stronger Than Life, Because He Loved Us with a Love Stronger Than Death!

The saying is trustworthy and deserving of full acceptance, that Christ Jesus came into the world to save sinners, of whom I am the foremost. (1 Timothy 1:15)

hrist's love for us was stronger than death. He died for love! He laid down his life to save our lives (see John 10:15, 17-18). He loves us just as the Father loves Him (see John 15:9). Oh, Scripture has extremely lofty words about His affection for us. Now, beloved, He died for us, and suffered for us, and set His heart on us to love and delight in us; then how we ought to love Him in return! *"You shall love the Lord your God with all your heart and with all your soul and with all your mind"* (Matthew 22:37; cf. Psalm 73:25 and 1 Peter 2:7).

Let your hearts be full of love and affection for Christ! Love will breed courage, and will throw out abject fear before God, and carnal fear before people. God can keep us from the torments of people, but people cannot keep us from the torments of God. While we stand by God, God has promised to stand by us; therefore, do not be afraid of any authority that stands in opposition to the authority of Christ!

No one can promise better than Christ can; no one can threaten us worse than Christ can. Can anyone threaten us with a worse thing than eternal hell? Can anyone promise us a better thing than eternal heaven? Heaven will be the inheritance of those who love Him, and hell will be the inheritance of those who hate Him.

My dear brothers, let us love Him with a love stronger than death, as did Paul and the rest of the apostles. *Who shall separate us from the love of Christ? Shall tribulation, or distress, or persecution, or famine, or nakedness, or danger, or sword?* (Romans 8:35). *Love is strong as death. . . . Many waters cannot quench love, neither can floods drown it* (Song of Solomon 8:6-7).

Chapter 20

Every day, Be As Serious in Your Preparations for Death, As If It Were Your Last Day

But God said to him, "Fool! This night your soul is required of you, and the things you have prepared, whose will they be?" (Luke 12:20).[17]

Just as no Christian knows when that final time and hour will be, also no wicked person knows when it will be. To live without the fear of death is to die living. To labor not to die is to labor in vain. People are afraid to die in such and such sins, but they are not afraid to live in such and such sins. Oh, the hell of horrors and terrors that await those souls who have their greatest work to do when they come to die! Therefore, prepare yourselves for death, so that you will be happy at death, and everlastingly blessed after death.

---

17   See also Job 14:14; Psalm 39:5-6; and James 4:14.

Did Christ not die for us so that we might live with Him? And shall we not desire to die and be with Him? A believer's dying day is his crowning day!

"Blessed are the dead who die in the Lord from now on." "Blessed indeed," says the Spirit, "that they may rest from their labors, for their deeds follow them!" (Revelation 14:13)

Oh, my brothers, I exhort you every day to spend some time in preparation for, and meditation on, death, judgment, hell, heaven, and eternity.

Eternity is a sum that can never be counted, a line that can never be measured! Eternity is a state of everlasting sorrow, or everlasting joy. Oh! Think on this, and prepare for this every day, before the night of death comes!

In Conclusion

A nd thus, my beloved, I have given you these twenty precious directions for your souls. I will leave this book with you as a product of my dearest love. My desire in all of this is your happiness here, and your blessedness hereafter.

My sincere and humble desire for you is that you would pay close attention to this book and my other written works – not only to read them, but also to reform your lives by them.

Oh, do your duty, live in your duty, and love your duty so that you may be converted, and be made partakers of the inheritance of Christians in glory. This is, and will be, the earnest and constant prayer of one who esteems it a most glorious privilege to be among the number of those *who follow the Lamb wherever he goes* (Revelation 14:4).

Appendix

Holy and Helpful Sayings
of William Dyer[18]

Many have the space of repentance who do not have the grace of repentance.

It's better to repent without perishing than to perish without repenting.

There is more bitterness resulting from the ending of sins than there ever was sweetness flowing from the committing of sins.

Love for Christ produces a hatred for sin; now, whoever does not love Christ above all, does not love Him at all.

---

18 The following compilation of quotations, as appended here, was originally published anonymously as a broadside (February 27, 1680), and titled, *Holy and Profitable Sayings of that Reverend Divine, Mr. William Dyer, Late Preacher of the Gospel at Chesham And Chouldsbury, in the County of Bucks.* (Online source: https://archive.org/details/bim_early-english-books-1641-1700_holy-and-profitable-sayi_dyer-william_1680.)

All of our precious mercies come swimming to us in precious blood.

Those who sow holiness in the seedtime of their lives will reap happiness in the harvest of eternity.

Swimming in the waterworks of repentance is better than burning in the fireworks of God's vengeance.

There is no coming to the fair haven of glory without sailing through the narrow strait of repentance.

If Christ had not freed us from the curse, we would have lived cursedly and died cursedly, and would have been damned forever.

Those who despise the death of the Lamb will surely feel the wrath of the Lamb.

Those who will not own Christ at His first coming, Christ will not own at His second coming.

He who came from heaven to make believers righteous will also come from heaven to make believers glorious. He is the rich jewel in the cabinet of glory.

Whoever has [Christ] cannot be poor, and whoever does not have Him cannot be rich.

Christians take as much delight in those doctrines that instruct holiness as they do in those promises that assure happiness.

If the day of mercy leaves you graceless, the day of judgment will find you speechless.

Justice enraged will avenge the quarrel of mercy abused. The longer God waits without finding amendment, the sorer He strikes when He comes to judgment.

If God's delaying mercy does not draw you to repentance, His judgment will drive you to destruction.

The sea of damnation will not be sweetened with a drop of compassion.

Just as you look for happiness so long as God has His existence in heaven, God also looks for holiness so long as you have your existence on earth.

Humans are the excellency of creatures. Christians are the excellency of humans. Grace is the excellency of Christians. And glory is the excellency of grace.

It is a greater kindness to be converted than to be created. Yes, it is far better to have no life, than to not have a new life.

Inward holiness is better than outward happiness.

Goodness without greatness is better than greatness without goodness.

Christ threw Himself into the sea of His Father's wrath to save poor believers from drowning.

He has shut the door of hell, rescued us from perdition, and He has opened the gate of heaven to let us into salvation.

Oh, how much is it the people's duty to serve God, since God has made all the world for that purpose?

If the life of Christ is not your influence, then the death of Christ will never be your inheritance.

The human soul is the cabinet, God's grace is the jewel; now, where Christ does not find the jewel, He will throw away the cabinet.

Wherever Christ is a priest for redemption, He is likewise a prince for dominion. Wherever He is a Savior, there He is a ruler. Where He is a fountain of happiness, there He is a fountain of holiness.

It is seldom seen that the sparkling diamond of a great estate is set in the gold ring of a gracious heart.

A sight of ourselves in grace will certainly bring us to a sight of ourselves in glory.

Those sins will never make a hell for us that are a hell to us, for where people are so diligent to do their best, God is so indulgent to forgive the worst.

To be in Christ is heaven below, and to be with Christ is heaven above.

Though holiness is that which a sinner scorns, yet holiness is that which a Savior crowns.

Similar Titles

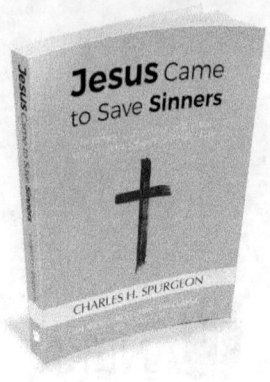

Jesus Came to Save Sinners,
by Charles H. Spurgeon

This is a heart-level conversation with you, the reader. Every excuse, reason, and roadblock for not coming to Christ is examined and duly dealt with. If you think you may be too bad, or if perhaps you really are bad and you sin either openly or behind closed doors, you will discover that life in Christ is for you too. You can reject the message of salvation by faith, or you can choose to live a life of sin after professing faith in Christ, but you cannot change the truth as it is, either for yourself or for others. As such, it behooves you and your family to embrace truth, claim it for your own, and be genuinely set free for now and eternity. Come and embrace this free gift of God, and live a victorious life for Him.

Available where books are sold.

The Pursuit of God, by A. W. Tozer

To have found God and still to pursue Him is a paradox of love, scorned indeed by the too-easily-satisfied religious person, but justified in happy experience by the children of the burning heart. Saint Bernard of Clairvaux stated this holy paradox in a musical four-line poem that will be instantly understood by every worshipping soul:

> *We taste Thee, O Thou Living Bread,*
> *And long to feast upon Thee still:*
> *We drink of Thee, the Fountainhead*
> *And thirst our souls from Thee to fill.*

Available where books are sold.

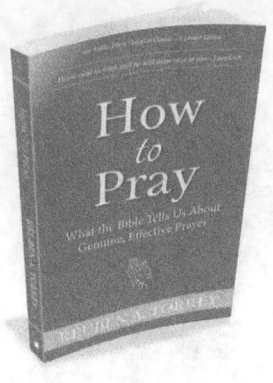

How to Pray, by Reuben A. Torrey

Prayer. Satan laughs as he looks at the church today and says to himself, "You can have your Sunday schools and your young people's small groups, your boys' and girls' programs, your vacation Bible schools, your Christian schools, your elegant churches, your retreats, your music programs, your brilliant preachers, and even your revival efforts – as long as you don't bring the power of almighty God into them by earnest, persistent, believing, mighty prayer."

Great revivals always begin first in the hearts of a few men and women whom God arouses by His Spirit to believe in Him as a living God, as a God who answers prayer, and upon whose heart He lays a burden from which no rest can be found except in persistent crying unto God.

Available where books are sold.

Total Commitment to Christ, by A. W. Tozer

I am the Light of the world; he who follows Me will not walk in the darkness, but will have the Light of life.
– John 8:12

Christians ought to be so totally committed to Christ that it is final. Of looking back over your shoulder to see if there is something better – let that never again be your experience.

A short but inspiring booklet on how to follow Christ with your whole heart.

Available where books are sold.